Aaron Edwin Penley

Sketching from nature in water-colours

Aaron Edwin Penley

Sketching from nature in water-colours

ISBN/EAN: 9783744640244

Printed in Europe, USA, Canada, Australia, Japan

Cover: Foto ©Thomas Meinert / pixelio.de

More available books at **www.hansebooks.com**

SKETCHING FROM NATURE

IN

WATER-COLOURS.

BY

AARON PENLEY,

AUTHOR OF "THE ENGLISH SCHOOL OF PAINTING IN WATER-COLOURS," "ELEMENTS OF PERSPECTIVE,"
"A SYSTEM OF PAINTING IN WATER-COLOURS,"
ETC. ETC.

WITH ILLUSTRATIONS IN CHROMO-LITHOGRAPHY AFTER
ORIGINAL WATER-COLOUR DRAWINGS.

CASSELL PETTER & GALPIN:
LONDON, PARIS & NEW YORK.

INTRODUCTION.

IN the present day, there is such an increasing love for water-colour Art, and such a wish for its attainment, that it is most desirable there should be every assistance afforded to the student, whereby he shall be enabled to carry it out with some little degree of certainty. Nature is so varied, and her effects so numberless, that it is impossible to present too many examples for her study. Nevertheless, although the range of subjects is unlimited, and the field for picturesque charms so ever recurrent, yet the treatment of landscape-painting can, without doubt, be disposed of in some methodical manner, by which a progressive execution can be made somewhat plain to most minds. Although much has been written upon the subject, yet there is much that needs to be written; and so, indeed, there always must be, from the fact of scenic representation being so inexhaustible. It will therefore be superfluous to offer any apology for introducing the following pages by way of instruction. The purport of the present work is to guide the sketcher in the use of his colours, as well as to point out the importance of good and truthful drawing, and, indeed, to present to him the means and the manner of the manipulation. Its object is also to create a love for Nature, by dwelling upon her beauties, and unfolding, to some extent, in what those beauties consist; while it affects to lead to a slight knowledge of the construction of a drawing, and how Art is brought to bear upon a scene, so as to impart to it an increased interest, and consequent loveliness.

The treatment of two of the illustrations is given in different stages of progression; but it is not intended that the work should be of such an elementary character as to assume that those who study from it are entirely ignorant of water-colour drawing. It rather supposes previous practice and tuition; and, under this impression, it introduces to the amateur subjects likely to lead him on to a more clear and definite comprehension as to how they are begun, continued, and brought to completion. There are no details left unnoticed that shall in any way leave the pupil in a state of uncertainty; yet it does not profess to give the power to colour and manipulate successfully without a corresponding effort of the mind on the part of the pupil, and a fair amount of practice. Both these there must be, as without them *nothing* can be achieved. They are indispensable.

I have great hope that the coloured examples in this present volume, and the full explanation given with each of them, will prove of great utility to the inquiring amateur, and that it will meet with that appreciation it has been my sincere study it should deserve.

CONTENTS.

The Colour Box.

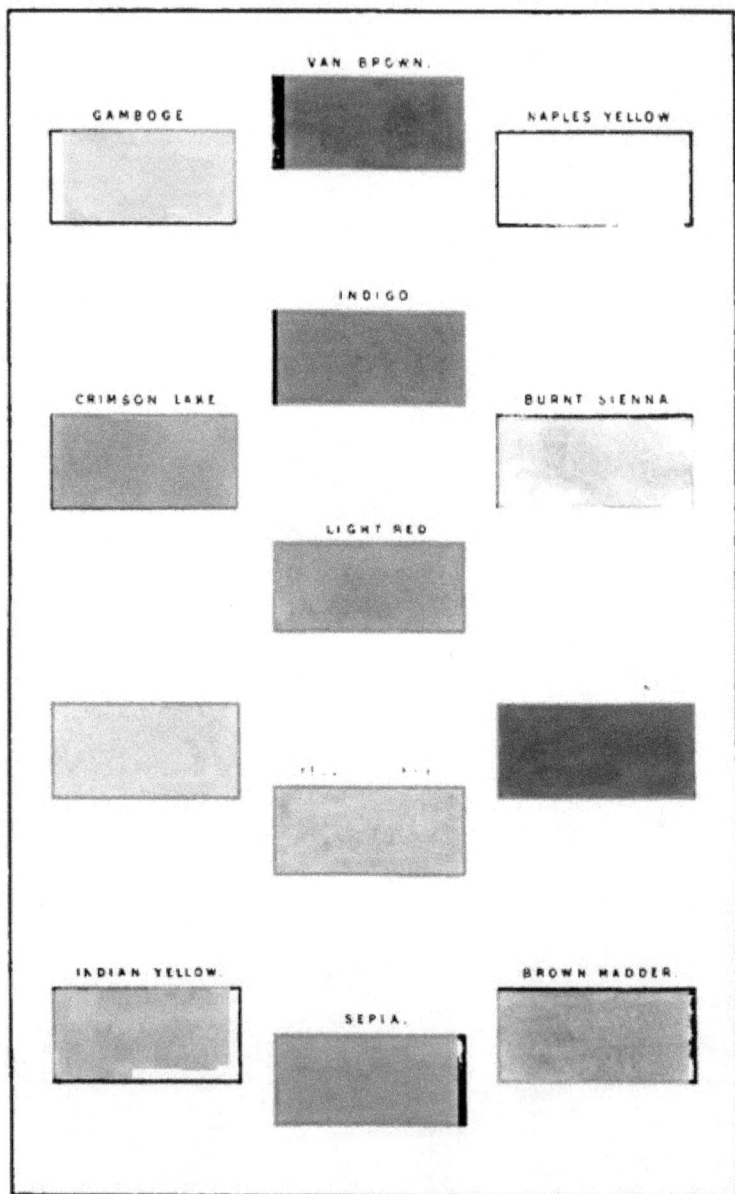

ON COLOURS, PAPER, AND BRUSHES.

FOR general use, when sketching from Nature, the fewer the colours to be employed the better, not only for the sake of simplicity, but also to give as light a weight and bulk as possible. I do not, however, recommend too small a box, nor half-sized colours, believing them to be a hindrance in affording that full supply of colour which, at times, is absolutely necessary to cover large spaces. And besides this, the box is so soon covered with divers tints, that it requires to be constantly cleansed and wiped that a succession of pure tones may be applied without being sullied or altered. It should be the sketcher's chief aim to copy very exactly the colour of every object presented, and to take cognizance of every deviation from that colour, it being of rare occurrence that it continues unchanged or unbroken; and to do this correctly, or, indeed, with any degree of pleasure, it is imperative that there shall be room enough upon the palette to mix the colours satisfactorily.

A box, therefore, containing 12 colours is such as to afford every opportunity for colouring out of doors, and with it a japanned water-bottle to hang on one end of the box. This must not be very small, and it is as well to work with a fair quantity of water, that it may not get dirty too soon.

To work with any degree of success and comfort, a good and convenient sketching-stool is essential. The hands should be at liberty, one to hold the colour-box and the other to wield the pencil; for if they are employed to support the paper also, they become trammelled and cramped, rendering it impossible to impart that freedom of execution which is the characteristic of an out-door drawing. I always use a folding stool, which, when opened, forms an easel and support for the drawing board or block. Nothing can be more complete than this, and they can be obtained at any of our artists' colourmen. The only drawback is the size and weight; but to most persons this will scarcely be deemed an objection, and more especially when on a sketching tour.

Another requisite is an umbrella, to keep the sun from the drawing, and so enable the artist to form a correct idea of what he is doing. It is almost impossible to judge of colour with the sun shining in all its whiteness upon the paper, and not only so, but it is absolutely injurious to the sight, frequently making the head ache severely. These umbrellas are mostly of holland, and have a long stick, with an iron point at one end and a screw at the other. They can be firmly stuck into the ground, and form an independent covering, and will protect from rain as well as sun.

Where the sketch is not large, a solid block of paper, made with Whatman's thick imperial, will, for most amateurs, be found the best. It should either be quarto or octavo: a larger size enhances the difficulty of the sketch, and a smaller size cramps the scene and the hand. Another convenient method of holding the paper is a mahogany board, having a number of little points all round, and with a slight frame, attached by hinges. The paper should be damped before being placed in it, when it becomes tightly strained and easy for working upon. Rough paper is by no means so favourable for the amateur as that of a medium texture. It resists the action of the brush, and will not receive the washes with that freedom or certainty that is desirable. The difficulty is quite great enough, without adding to it. For this reason, I prefer the thick imperial to the thin; there being more texture and a greater substance, the washes of colour do not dry up so quickly in warm or windy weather. This quick drying is a great evil, and at times it is almost impossible to succeed in giving clear, large tones for the sky and clouds. I know of no better plan to remedy this than by damping the paper, and taking the water off again with clean blotting-paper, of which there should always be a supply.

The rough paper (ninety pounds to the ream) is excellent, and very suitable for taking capital washes, and also for obtaining a certain quality, from the fact of the surface being granular and receiving the colours kindly. It is not so coarse as the thick paper, while it holds the tints in a damp state quite as

B

long, and is far easier to be touched upon. Care, however, must be taken to procure it of a moderate degree of roughness, as it varies much in this respect.

The thick double elephant is also most useful, and, like the thick imperial, works extremely well, retaining the moisture longer than the smoother and thinner papers. The antiquarian is, perhaps, the best paper we have for the studio. It is exquisitely even in grain, and capable of the highest degree of finish. The thickness is not sufficient to prevent its cockling; but this can, and indeed should, always be remedied by first straining another piece of paper and then laying it down by means of paste. If this is properly done, the antiquarian paper is certainly very good.

In speaking of papers, of course much must depend upon the style and manner of the sketcher. Some may be extremely careful in their drawing, attending to every detail, and thus produce a faithful rendering of the scene. Others may be so charmed with colour as to be induced to generalise the accuracy of the drawing, and only represent their impression of the landscape, by some peculiarities of harmonising and contrasting tones. Many, doubtless, will combine the two without neglecting either, and thereby transmit to their papers the most agreeable and recognisable effect. It matters but little in what style the drawing is made, provided that the mind has been employed upon the work, and a due share of careful handling has been exhibited. A careless and slovenly manner borders upon conceit, and invariably fails of conveying any idea of the place represented, while it calls forth remarks that must be anything but pleasing to the student who has been guilty of such a performance. It is to be hoped that this may prove a caution to those who may not have duly considered the importance of "*taking pains*" with all they do.

PENCILS AND BRUSHES.

The H B and B blacklead pencils are by far the best for sketching from Nature. They are sufficiently soft to enable the hand to move freely, and hard enough to prevent their smudging. Should the paper be rough, the F pencil will be found useful. When the pencil sketch is made, it is a good plan to wash a very slight tint of neutral orange all over it. This will, in some measure, fix and secure it from being rubbed.

The brushes to be employed should be of black sable hair. They retain their points and hold together when filled with colour far better than others.

A large flat brush is useful for wetting the paper all over, and also for washing; but I do not approve of it for giving a coat of colour.

For large washes, the swan quill is the best that can be used, and more especially in producing the first tints of the sky and distances; but, as a general rule, it will be found to hold too much colour for the more detailed parts of a drawing.

All forms that require to be given with individual character should be manipulated with the small swan or goose quill. These sizes are large enough to produce washes of some pretensions, while they do not confuse the draughtsman by an overcharge of colour. It is a matter of some import, and that the hand should be enabled to master the brush, and not the brush to master the hand.

Smaller brushes are seldom required, except for the purpose of painting in figures, and even then they should never be too small, as there is always a want of fulness and force in the colours imparted.

I generally use the sable brushes made in the Albata ferrules, with black handles. They are firm to hold and more convenient to carry.

In addition to these, a goose-quill size and one still smaller are required. These also may be procured in the Albata ferrules.

THE COLOUR BOX.

Gamboge.	Indian Yellow.	Light Red.	Naples Yellow.*	Vermilion.*
Crimson Lake.	Vandyck Brown.	Yellow Ochre.	Burnt Sienna.	Brown Madder.
Cobalt.	Indigo.	Sepia.		

The above will be found calculated to meet all the requirements of most sketches, and if more colours are necessary, they might be carried loosely and used occasionally. The following may be obtained for this

* Half-pans of each.

purpose :—Chinese White (in tube or bottle), Lemon Yellow, Raw Sienna, Cadmium, Aureolin, Neutral Orange, Rose Maddor, Purple Madder, Brown Pink, French Blue, Oxide of Chromine, Burnt Umber, Viridian, Orange Vermilion, Blue Black. It will be seen that rather a large number has been added; but as all will be mentioned in detail, it was better to enumerate them here.

CHINESE WHITE.

A permanent White of much body. It works extremely well, both in thin washes and thick touches, and mixes with every colour in the most agreeable manner. An abuse of it is much to be guarded against.

NAPLES YELLOW.

An opaque light Yellow, rather broken in tone. It is of much service in extreme distances, in sunset skies, on buildings, and for mixing with other colours for the production of foliage tints, either bright or subdued. It gives tones that cannot be obtained without it. Cobalt, Rose Madder, and Naples Yellow, yield a variety of soft aërial Greys.

LEMON YELLOW.

A pure colour, as its name implies. It is extremely powerful, and must be employed with caution. Sunny gleams owe much of their vividness to this colour. Mixed with a little Viridian, it gives rich, bright, and unsullied Greens.

CADMIUM.

A deep and powerful Yellow, of much body. Where great luminous force is sought, nothing is so calculated to give it, even to a metallic lustre. Useful in skies, distances, coloured objects, and drapery. Its permanence may be relied upon.

AUREOLIN.

A remarkably pure Yellow, full in colour, with plenty of body, and is suited for every Green tint. Works admirably, is very permanent, and of great service in Water-colour Painting.

RAW SIENNA.

A broken Yellow, of much warmth and beauty. By many this colour is highly esteemed, and deservedly so. It is an exquisite glazing colour, but does not work agreeably in tree-painting, owing to its being rather slimy when used with some intensity. With Lake, it gives Orange tones of a most transparent kind.

YELLOW OCHRE.

Of all the Yellows, none are so useful for landscape-painting as this. By itself, it is a broken Yellow, and often in request as a tone to the paper. It compounds well with every colour, and, in combination with Cobalt and Lake, it produces almost every variety of Grey. These tints are equally suited for clouds, mountains, water, distances of every description, buildings, rocks, banks, sands, roads, old wood, cattle, figures, and, indeed, everything except trees, for which purpose it is too thick and murky, wanting in brilliancy, transparency, and freshness. Permanent.

INDIAN YELLOW.

Most useful in foliage painting. It gives rich and soft Greens of some body. Being slightly opaque, it may be used very thickly, and still look light. With Indigo and Burnt Sienna, it produces most desirable tree colours; is also of much use in figures and coloured objects.

GAMBOGE.

An indispensable colour for foliage and herbage in general. It yields every description of Green, pure and broken. With Burnt Sienna and Indigo, we have the most useful range of Greens for trees possible. By substituting Vandyck Brown for Burnt Sienna, the tints are cooler, and again for Sepia, still cooler.

In mixture with Sepia alone, we have hues of great beauty and softness. Gamboge, Lake, and Indigo afford every variety of Grey Greens for shadows. Gamboge, Lake, and Cobalt, with a little Yellow Ochre, are mostly employed for foliage in the middle distance. Grass and weeds of every kind may be treated with these same colours; Indigo being for the foreground and Cobalt for the distance. Unfortunately, it is not a permanent colour; and yet, as in tree-painting it is used in some power, it may be adopted without much fear of change.

NEUTRAL ORANGE.

Is extremely useful for washing over the whole drawing previous to commencing the colouring. It gives a luminous character to the paper, and acts upon the subsequent air tones with considerable effect and truthfulness, giving to them a subdued softness of tone. With Cobalt or French Blue, it produces a greenish Grey, adapted both for distances and foregrounds. Is very permanent.

BURNT SIENNA.

A broken, transparent Orange colour, and one of the most generally useful colours we have. It enters into the composition of almost every tint for landscape, and, either in its lightest washes or deepest touches, will be found equally desirable. No box is perfect without it, as it possesses a quality, both as to tone and texture, that is indispensable. It were invidious to enumerate its uses in detail, as it is in constant demand.

CHINESE ORANGE.

Much the same as Burnt Sienna, only more brilliant in tone, and, when given in intensity, is certainly extremely powerful. Permanent.

LIGHT RED.

Most useful, either by itself or in combination with other colours. Is most adapted for air tones when mixed with Cobalt, French Blue, or Indigo. Well suited for all warm Greys for roads, banks, and buildings.

VENETIAN RED.

Rather more Laky in tone than Light Red, but very useful in every stage of a drawing.

INDIAN RED.

A powerful and deep colour, yielding strong Grey tones for dark clouds and deep shadows. There are times when the intensity of purply Greys in mountain regions cannot be approached without it, in mixture with Indigo. As, however, it is inclined to heaviness, it is as well to use it with caution, especially as it eats up the other colours with which it is compounded.

BROWN MADDER.

A transparent, broken Red, somewhat partaking of the Indian Red tone. It is one of the finest colours we have for admixture with others for landscape Greys, also for deep, warm tones on buildings, banks, &c. With Indigo it is most useful, and with Cobalt exquisitely tender; with Sepia it yields tones of great utility, and with any of the Yellows many splendid and natural autumnal tints are obtained. It works most kindly, and is considered permanent.

ORANGE VERMILION.

A bright Orange Scarlet, opaque and powerful. Is in repute for coloured objects and draperies. With a little Chinese White, it is admirable for the faces, hands, and feet for small figures, causing them to hold out with vividness. Is occasionally used in the Orange tones of a sunset sky.

VERMILION.

Indispensable when required. With Cobalt, it gives strong Greys, and by itself, in light tints, is most favourable for imparting a certain beauty and warmth over parts of the sky and distances, water, &c. It was in great repute with Turner, who frequently used it quite pure for his shadows in many parts of a picture. When employed with judgment and care, it certainly is truly exquisite, and, as its permanence is undisputed, there should be no hesitation in adopting it. Being a heavy colour, it precipitates when used with other colours, unless laid on quickly.

ROSE MADDER.

A most beautiful and delicate Crimson, of great service in all tender tones, whether in Greys or in local colours. On account of its permanence, it is indispensable for the soft air tones of clouds, water, and distances, and quite supersedes the Crimson Lake for these purposes. When any great power is required, it is not adapted to give it, the Crimson Lake being far better and fuller in quality.

CRIMSON LAKE.

Of immense value in almost every part of a drawing, and is necessary for every kind of Grey, warm or cold. Its want of permanence does not render it safe for light tones; but this is of little consequence, as Rose Madder can fulfil these requirements. It enters considerably into all deep tones for shadows, and more particularly those that are transparent. With Brown Pink, it is most admirable for deep touches, as also with Burnt Sienna and Indigo, Cobalt, or French Blue. With Gamboge and Lake, it makes soft Grey tones for the shadows of trees.

PURPLE MADDER.

A rich Brown Purple, of great permanence and power. It yields exquisitely soft Greys for clouds, water, and distances, as well as for Grey shadows generally, while it is equally useful in foreground painting, and for figures and cattle.

COBALT.

In more request than any other colour. As Blue forms the principal ingredient in Greys, and as Cobalt more nearly resembles the character of distance, so does this colour enter into every description of tone and tint, from the middle distance to the sky. It will, therefore, be needless to say more about it, other than that it is always in use, and has to be replenished in the colour box very frequently, whilst many other colours may remain on hand for years.

FRENCH BLUE.

Bright, powerful, and useful. By some, this is in greater request than Cobalt; but for general purposes it will be found too strong, neither does it unite so kindly with other colours. There is, nevertheless, a lustre about it far exceeding that of the Cobalt, and at times is much more truthful in the aërial tones it imparts. In soft Grey gloom, nothing can be more effective, or give a greater impression of mystery in the mid-distant breadths of shade. It may be used instead of Indigo or Cobalt for tree-painting, also for coloured objects and drapery.

INDIGO.

Foreground foliage and herbage claim this colour as especially belonging to them, while the deep-toned Browns, Greys, and Purples depend upon its presence. For landscape purposes it holds a very high rank in every list of colours, and is much appreciated by every artist. It is impossible to do without it. Unfortunately it is not quite permanent; but is the best Blue of the kind at present known.

PRUSSIAN BLUE.

A bright and transparent Blue; but little used in landscape-painting, on account of its being fugitive.

BLUE BLACK.

A fine toned Black, useful for black objects and cattle, also for reducing the brightness of many colours, by imparting greater softness, and lowering them in tone.

VANDYCK BROWN.

A warm and rich Brown, of much service in foreground painting, whether for Greys, Browns, or deep shadows. It is also an excellent colour for tree-painting, with Gamboge and Indigo.

c

BURNT UMBER.

A soft, warm Brown. With Cobalt, it yields soft Greys, of a Greenish hue, and with Brown Madder, or Lake and Cobalt, will produce many admirable tones for buildings, banks, rocks, &c., and also for other foreground purposes. Is much esteemed by many water-colour painters.

SEPIA.

A fine, deep, and soft Brown, working most kindly, and mixing perfectly with other colours. With Rose Madder and Cobalt, it affords Greys of fine tone, suited for clouds, light or dark, and also distances, rocks, water, and other objects. Payne's Grey is a compound of Sepia, Lake, and Indigo. With Gamboge, it is most useful for trees, and, with Brown Madder and Indigo, is capital in its variety of tints for buildings, boats, rocks, roads, wood, and almost all foreground objects. Permanent.

VIRIDIAN.

A colour of great purity, brilliancy, and transparency, and may be used with advantage whenever any Greens of lustrous quality are required. It modifies the Cobalt by imparting a peculiar tone to it, and will often be found extremely advantageous to many of the purer Green portions of a drawing. Very well adapted for drapery and painted objects. Is permanent.

OXIDE OF CHROMINE.

A powerful and opaque Green. Serviceable to the landscape-painter for foliage and herbage, and more particularly when any of the shadows are put on too heavily. This, with a little Indian Yellow, or Naples Yellow, will clear up the parts, which may afterwards be glazed upon with transparent Yellow and Blue to regain the required freshness. Permanent.

TERRE VERTE.

A soft Green, of thin quality. Useful as a glazer, by imparting a sweetness of tone that is so often to be found in Nature. It is rather cool in tone, and by many artists is in great request for distances and foliage.

CERULEAN BLUE.

A Blue somewhat of a Greener hue than Cobalt. It certainly has peculiar charms of its own, and for distances is sometimes exquisite in effect. Being a very powerful colour, it should only be used to finish with, as Cobalt is preferable for the first washes.

We can speak very favourably of the colours that are supplied by the Artists' Colourmen. There is, as a rule, little or no imperfection in the material offered, so that there is nothing to prevent the artist from giving every effect of which colour is capable, whether in its extreme softness and delicacy, its richness of colour, both pure and broken, or its transparent brilliancy and depth of intensity. For permanency, for firmness of texture, evenness of flowing in flat washes, freedom from deposit or any gelatinous and slimy nature, readiness for use, perfection in numberless combinations, and freshness of tone, it is impossible to wish for any improvement in the colours: they have reached the highest degree of excellence to which they can be brought.

GROUP OF FIR TREES, DRAWN FROM NATURE.

THIS plate is extremely simple in character, consisting only of a group of Fir Trees, the like of which may be met with in almost every belt or plantation of the same species. It was drawn upon the spot, and selected for the clear manner in which the light and shadow were developed, giving to each branch, or portion of it, an individuality peculiarly its own, and yet so expressed as to favour breadth of effect and harmony in the entire group. Such "bits" or "studies" require but little time to produce, although nothing can be more useful or profitable than a sketch-book filled with sketches of the different classes of trees.

I much recommend the practice of carefully and freely drawing each tree with the blacklead pencil, especially with reference to the main stems, noticing well their direction or inclination from the perpendicular, and how the several lines affect each other in giving a graceful disposition of *form*, because it is only by a due observance of these combinations that an impression of elegance and refinement can be conveyed. It is a matter of importance to the general effect, that the bearings of the principal lines should be studied and remarked upon. For instance, it is as well to note, if the perpendicular stem of one tree be accompanied by that of another that is taking an angle or curve in a certain direction, what influence the change of line has upon the eye; whether it is, or is not, too abrupt; or if the two compose so agreeably as to give a pleasing effect. I like much to linger before groups of trees, young or old, whether clothed or not clothed with foliage, and by change of position to see the many varieties of forms they take, and which of the many would produce the most pleasing composition. There is real pleasure in this—much to be learnt and much to be put in practice. Lessons may be had in many localities whence lessons could scarcely be expected to be gleaned, and our daily converse with a commonplace scene may be thus fraught with increased interest and pleasure.

The ability to draw naturally leads to observation of detail and generalisation, it being evident that this cannot be exercised without a corresponding reflection upon everything presented, as to construction, growth, character, and use. How far this is desirable, every one must judge for himself. I can only say that to myself the enjoyment is beyond expression; and often, when walking over what would be considered a monotonous and dreary plain, with a canopy of dull, leaden clouds, I am struck with beautiful undulating lines, varieties of tone and tint, with receding distances and aërial perspective, that produce much to be admired, thought upon, and studied. The infinitude of Nature demands the highest mental exercise and the perfection of Art, and we only are to blame if we do not see in her every phase something (I would rather say everything) from which to glean instruction, and to derive contemplative pleasure.

In writing thus, it must be clearly understood that the motive is to lead *others* to exercise a similar attention to Nature in her generality, and not to suppose that it is only upon scenes of grandeur and acknowledged loveliness that our admiration should be called forth. Doubtless the character of such favoured spots is calculated, from its exquisite combinations, to arrest the attention of the most unobservant, but it is also from every description and feature of landscape, as well as from various accidental groupings of figures, cattle, trees, buildings, vessels, &c., that the lover of Nature and drawing should derive constant delight combined with instruction. Something can be gathered from all we see, if the information conveyed be really sought for.

In commencing the outline of the present group of trees, the central stem should be drawn first, noticing carefully the direction of inclination from a perpendicular line. This *must* be correct. After this, give the stem nearest to it to the right, placing a dot at the proper distance for the bottom, and another for the top. By this plan the lines cannot fail of being in true position. The tree to the left must follow, by placing the dots both for the bottom and central part of the stem at its junction with the lower cluster of foliage; then the branches from its right side. The outer stem to the left may also be drawn after the same manner, and afterwards that to the right, with the several leading branches; those more receding can now easily be adjusted, by observing the direction in which they lean.

Further on, in the view of Grasmere, I have given instructions for drawing trees, precisely after the same manner as above; but it is desirable for pupils that the method of producing outlines should be constantly brought before them.

The foliage of the nearest and central tree should have its several forms and clusters completed first; then the tree to the left; and afterwards the small one to the right, as well as the rest of them mingling behind. In the original drawing the whole of the shadows were *pencilled* in firmly and distinctly, with close and rather long lines, but the distant shades were more loosely given. In sketching from Nature, it is always as well to adopt the most ready means of producing the effect, for which I find the assistance of pencilled shadows extremely serviceable.

When the shadows are finished, and the several characteristics of the stems, with their limbs and knotty projections, are correctly placed, the colours may be introduced, by washing them in without hesitation, not being too particular to take them up to the exact markings of the outline. This, indeed, has to be avoided, to prevent stiffness or the semblance of solidity, instead of multiplicity of leafage.

In the example, the sky was washed in at the last, in order that the lights might be so placed as to render the effect agreeable, as well as valuable to the group, and give (what should always be sought) breadth. All the colours were put on in rather a liquid condition, and the brush so filled as to impart them freely, without being blotchy or overcharged. It is a good plan to try the colours first upon a spare piece of paper, to judge of the tint, and practise the manner of touching before proceeding with the drawing. This will insure a greater chance of success.

Colours to be employed,—for the

SKY—Cobalt.

CLOUDS—Cobalt, sepia, and a very little lake.

FOLIAGE—Gamboge, indigo, lake; but the trees behind must have cobalt added, to give a more vapoury tune.

The colours mentioned above are to be used in combination, taking more or less of one than of the others, as the character of the tones may require.

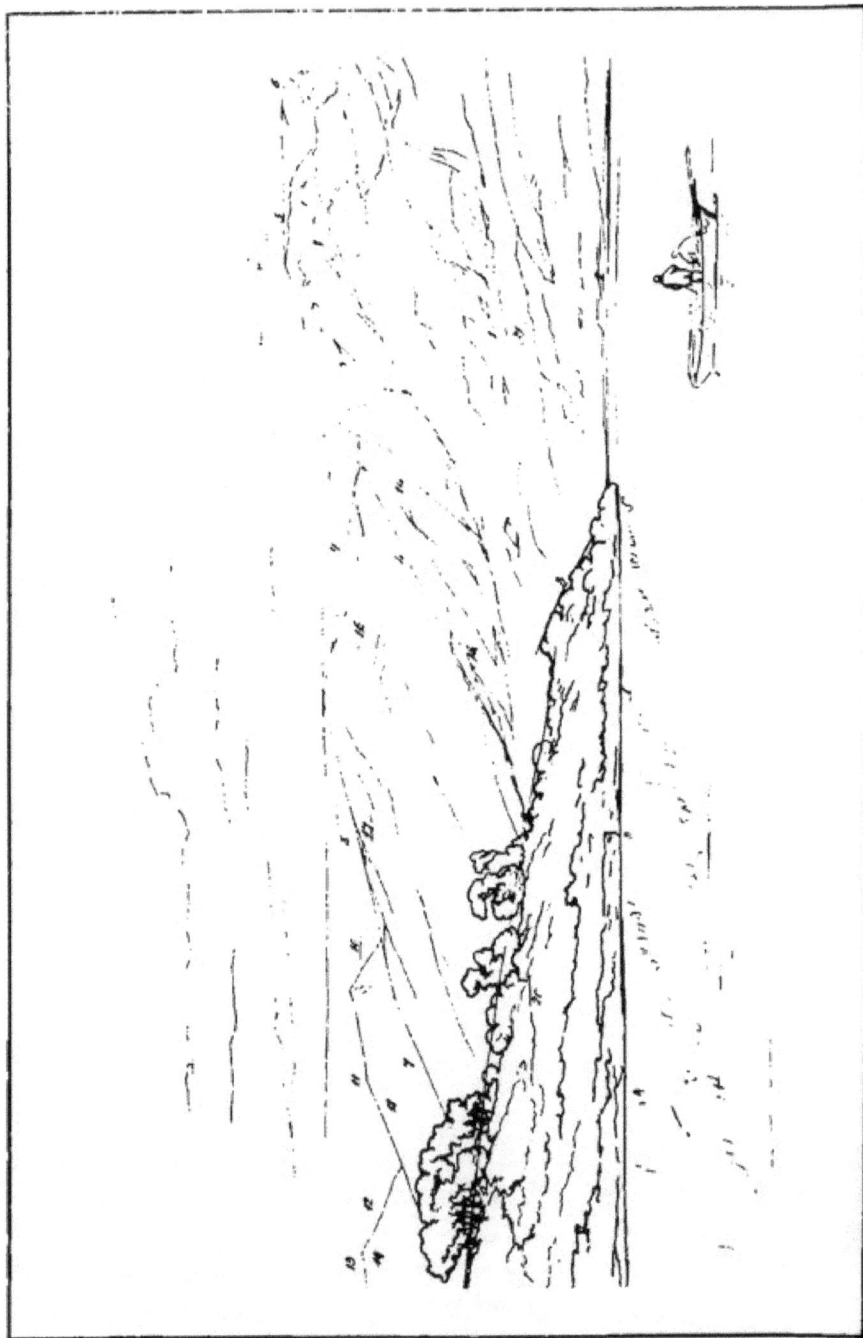

ON LOCH LOMOND.

IN introducing to the notice of the reader the following hints for sketching from Nature, I must be clearly understood as by no means pretending to have discovered any "royal road" to the acquisition of the whole art and mystery of water-colour painting. Like the poet, the painter must, I apprehend, be "*born*, not *made*;" and not even the most naturally gifted, as respects taste and intelligence, may hope to attain to more than a moderate skill without such a devotion of time as the successful pursuit of every other profession requires of those who embrace it. There are, however, thousands of those who take their pleasure by hill and river, who have neither the poetic "afflatus," nor the aspiration to be professed artists; and to whom a rudimentary knowledge of sketching in colour would be a highly-prized acquirement. To such as these I now address myself.

Apart from its utility, there is perhaps no accomplishment more to be desired than the ability to sketch from Nature, and so to transfer to paper, when opportunity offers, some of her choicest scenes. It gives an additional zest to travel, and adds, in a peculiar manner, to the intelligent traveller's store of information. For it is impossible to put pencil to paper without being struck by the perfection and completeness of objects before us; and we can imitate none of Nature's forms without an elevating appreciation of their character, construction, and purpose. ART should ever go hand in hand with NATURE, to which it should attach itself closely, as to an infallible guide. Every principle of Art is dictated by, and drawn from *Nature*; and, so soon as the hand of the guide is dropped, *Art* will, I submit, cease to excite and gratify the intelligence of a Nature-loving student. This proposition I think none will assail; all, indeed, must acquiesce in it. The first precept, therefore, I would address to my student reader is, that, however slight a sketch from Nature may be, it must be a faithful transcript of the scene or object sketched, without conventionality of any kind.

A "sketch from Nature" should imply such a representation of the scene as will give a general impression of it without over much detail, and yet without any such omission as might alter the character or injure the effect produced on the mind. But to secure this generalisation without loss of resemblance, an educated eye, a practised hand, and a thorough knowledge of the forms under treatment, are necessary. A "study from Nature" is a different thing, demanding the strictest attention to every part, with literal truthfulness in the whole as well as in each part.

The first thing to be determined in a sketch is the position of the HORIZONTAL LINE. This must be faintly drawn across the paper, and the lines of every object above or below, and not parallel to it, must incline to some point on it. Of course, a certain knowledge of PERSPECTIVE is essential, and the student must acquire it before he can hope to sketch successfully.

To sketch in the outline correctly, it is necessary to observe very attentively the peculiar angles and position of the several objects to be drawn, in order that a truthful direction may be given to every line. All forms deviating from right lines—horizontal and perpendicular—assume certain angles, and upon a just appreciation of these angles the whole correctness of character must depend.

The relative position of the various objects in the field of view being once indicated (first lines should only be "indications"), the undulations or broken outlines, that certain of them may present, should be given, great care being taken against exaggeration,—an error of constant occurrence. It is not sufficient to give the outside lines only, because these are almost always the result of irregularities of surface, which claim to be themselves represented by lines of their own. For instance, the broken character of a mountain's top or side is due to the several masses of rock rearing their rugged heads at different elevations. These masses—if of any size, and in light—should be made to show whence they spring, and thus to express the actual character, or, as I may say, *construction* of the entire mountain. Character of surface, again, is requisite to give character of distance. A little eminence protruding from a mass often tells, with immense power, by throwing the more distant scenery far—very far—backward. Unfortunately, amateurs too often undertake to sketch subjects beyond their power; and, in the attempt to take in a multiplicity of objects, lose patience, become careless, and so end by giving but a vague idea of the landscape. Far better would it be to divide the scene, and to make three sketches instead of one.

D

The best class of subjects for beginners is, without doubt, to be found in the *lake* or *mountain* districts —at any rate, as far as outline is concerned,—because the principal objects there are few in number, and of large proportions; and in lake scenery, the straight line of water at the mountain's base is of the greatest value to the young sketcher as a guide to the position of objects whose lines rise from it. But, in order to give a clearer insight into the process of sketching, I give a skeleton sketch, with the coloured drawing, and claim the student's attention to the numbers by which each line is indicated on the latter, and would recommend the adoption of the plan in all sketches of a similar kind.

I have selected my subject for its simplicity. It is composed of only four separate masses, and these are so arranged as to afford a variety of angles, as well as of quantities—no two being alike. Repetition of forms, or rather direction of lines and sameness of quantity or size, should always be avoided; and with this view the artist frequently alters his position. The same scene, from different points of view, will assume quite a different composition; therefore, the manner in which the several lines constituting the forms come together should be most carefully studied; and a point should be selected by the sketcher whence they appear to have the most graceful bearing, and to intersect each other, without violent contrasts, at the angles.

In the outline sketch, the line No. 1 is the water-line, and is continued across the paper; 2, a waterline above it, giving the base of the mountain on the right hand; 3, the angles of the promontory; 4, the angle of the direction of the side of the near mountain; 5 and 6, the angles of the summit; 7, the angle of the central mountain from the point over the promontory; 8, change of angle to the top; 9, also a change of direction to the right, notice being taken of its exact incidence upon the line 4; 10 and 11 give the angles of the next mountain; 12 and 13 show the most distant hill. O is an imaginary line drawn horizontally across the top of the central mountain as a guide for the relative heights of the others; and it is important this should be strictly observed. After these lines of direction and position are correctly placed, the undulating and broken outlines (also numbered) are to be given with precision; seeing that each line represents the character of the rock, and the slope of the different surfaces: as, for example, in the broken ground of the promontory, the trees at its top edge, and the rising ground at the base of the near mountain to the right.

If attention be paid to the method by which these several lines follow in succession, much less difficulty will be experienced in any after sketches. The boat was put in to fill the vacant space in the water, and as a balance to the drawing.

The pencil outline being complete, it will be better to fix it by washing the drawing with plain water, or a slight wash of yellow ochre and lake, or neutral orange. Cobalt alone is employed for the sky, and is taken over the distant mountains and top of the near one. A tint of cobalt and lake, with a little yellow ochre, is then passed over the distant mountains, and changed for the nearer hill and crags to yellow ochre and lake, with a small portion of cobalt to check the brightness of the orange tone. Yellow ochre alone is used for the base and upper portion of the water, and changed again to cobalt about midway to the bottom of the drawing.

The whole of the paper being covered, the various shadows are to be introduced in the distance, and also on the large portions of crag on the right. Cobalt, lake, and yellow ochre are used, in different degrees; and the warm light tones washed in over the shadows. Raw umber, gamboge, cobalt, and lake are the colours for the herbage on the promontory, and are put on with a tint of much power, changing the character of tone where required. The different colours of the broken and rocky surface are glazed over the groundwork of grey previously laid on. The white bits of stone at the water's edge are most useful in causing the eye to fall on that part of the drawing, thereby giving a breadth to the whole of the half-tones above, and preventing the gleam of light on the near mountain from being a spot. For this purpose also, the spots of light at the edge and top of the lower range of crag on the right are serviceable in drawing the attention and giving value to the bright tones of the slopes covered with sunburnt grass and heather. The water is simply cobalt in a straight wash, and for the darker lines a little yellow ochre and lake are to be added. If the fingers be placed over the boat, the sketch will be seen to want interest, and the weight of colour to the left and in the deep shadows of the rocks to the right will be excessive. It was therefore necessary to overpower these by some object of greater strength and by a little bright colour. The white, again, gives tone to the surface of the water by its colourless contrast. For the bright yellow tints, gamboge is employed; and for the red tones, gamboge with lake or rose madder.

GLENFINLAS.

THE accompanying drawing is taken from the entrance of Glenfinlas, near the Brig of Turk and the Trosachs, and is selected as my second subject for its extreme simplicity of character, because I see in it a great variety of broad masses of *form*, combining, as it does, mountain, moorland, and a rudely picturesque Highland hut. The scene is given, exactly as I saw it, without addition or alteration. Indeed, there was no need for either, as every object was calculated to compose agreeably, and to produce a pleasing result. Nothing can exceed the charm of colour frequently found on old thatch. The patches of different grasses growing to seed upon it exhibit every description of tint; while the weather-stricken thatch itself assumes indefinite compounds of russet, brown, and purple greys. It is from such little "bits" that the artist gleans much knowledge of harmonising and natural blending, enabling him to bring the force of his palette into action, and yet keep clear of unpleasant or crude brightness. The lines of the cottage are broken by the position of several poles leaning against the roof; and as these have neither similarity in direction, nor equi-distance from one another, they present no stiffness or apparent *design*. There is also great diversity in the sloping roof; not only as regards colour, but also in its several layers or demarcations, which help to make up an agreeable, although broken, whole; while the chimney, with its slaty top, gives a point of darkness and intensity. The peat at the side of the cottage is well placed for giving depth of shade and warmth of colour. Such scenes as this the amateur should seek for his pencil; because, the component objects being few in number, there is little difficulty in dealing with them without confusion, or in tracing the manner in which the combinations of colours are effected. A far-off mountain, backed by light and flying clouds; a middle distance of broken undulating moorland; a cottage by the roadside, based by patches of grass; a large fragment or two of stone; a stone wall; and three small trees, compose the whole of the scene before us; with the exception of the horse and cart, which are introduced to convey *action, force,* and *interest.* The mountain is beautiful in form, and its rugged outline desirable, to prevent formality. It is also so placed with one of its sides warm, and the other cool in tone, as to receive a breadth of light and shadow. The lines of the middle distance, being curved in different directions, assist very naturally to give elevation and dignity to it; and the warm citrine yellow tone, with purple and laky heather, serve to send it far away into aërial grey. There is often much difficulty in giving expression to a large mass of moorland or hillside, unless the surface is extremely irregular; and, even then, we are not made cognizant of those features of character so requisite to portray, until some sudden gleam of sunshine lights up the more prominent parts, or, on the other hand, some passing clouds produce dark and telling divisions by their cast shadows.

I would deeply recommend all whose pencil is employed on moorland scenery, to notice the several undulations, and in what direction they continue, and where they terminate. It will be upon a correct disposition of these lines that distances will depend; for it is not unusual that several miles of space have to be expressed upon what would appear to a casual observer nothing more than a flat surface void of interest. When alluding to the charming and varied effects of moors and downs, I would recall to memory the exquisite productions of Copley Fielding; because many of them are truly beautiful, and exhibit a most poetic and refined feeling for Nature and Art.

In the present drawing, there is, in point of colour, great simplicity, harmony, and contrast, with a broad effect of daylight. The sky and clouds are cool and light in tint. The distant mountain rises with much tenderness of tone, deepening towards the extreme outline. Opposed to this is the citrine or yellow-tinged moorland, with its delicate markings and shadows of warm russet purples; the yellows causing the greys to appear more aërial, and the half-toned shadows throwing the mass far into distance. The local tones of the motley-coloured roof, poles, and stone walls, give a soft appearance to the mass of moorland, placing it at once in the middle distance. And, again, the broad grey shadow of the cottage side gives an increase of vigour to the local colours. The brightest lights in the drawing will be found on the cottage wall, it being requisite that these should be clear and attractive. Next in degree of light is the road, with the intervals between the patches of grass, and so diffused as to cause the eye to regard the whole of the foreground. The shadows of the stone wall to the left, and across the road, connect the sides of the drawing, and repeat the tones of grey dispersed throughout it. For this purpose also, the shadows on the fragments of rock are of much service, as well as those of a warm colour. The cart is so placed as to repeat the tone of the stone wall; and the black horse, to give a point of concentration; while the colour of the figures subdues the whole. The position of the trees, encircling the subject with their deep and broken greens, is also valuable.

The colours employed were, for the

SKY—Cobalt.

CLOUDS—Cobalt, sepia, and a little lake.

MOUNTAIN—Cobalt, lake; yellow ochre, shaded with cobalt and lake; a light wash of raw sienna and lake on the top, and of terre verte on the lower part.

MOORLAND OR MIDDLE DISTANCE—A wash of yellow ochre and raw sienna over the whole. For the markings of shadows and forms, raw sienna, cobalt and lake; after which a few glazings of raw sienna and lake, and of terre verte in the green shades between the several markings.

COTTAGE ROOF AND POLES—Cobalt, lake, and raw sienna; sepia being added for the deep shadows and markings.

COTTAGE WALL IN SHADOW—Sepia, lake, and cobalt.

PEAT—Brown madder for the lights, and brown madder and sepia for the shadows.

GRASS—Gamboge, burnt sienna, and indigo.

TREES—Gamboge, burnt sienna, and indigo, in some depth of colour.

SHADOW ON ROAD—Sepia, lake, and indigo; a little gamboge added for the stone wall.

SHADOWS OF LARGE STONES—Sepia, lake, and indigo, with a glazing of terre verte.

COLOUR OF THE ROAD—Yellow ochre, a little lake, and sepia.

WARM STONES—Yellow ochre and lake.

CART—Sepia and yellow ochre, shaded with sepia, lake, and indigo.

FIGURE—Lake, shaded with sepia.

HORSE—Sepia, lake and indigo.

STONES ON THE COTTAGE WALL—Modification of raw sienna, lake, cobalt, and sepia.

THE FIRST PEEP OF GRASMERE FROM THE KESWICK ROAD.

———◦◦◦◦◦———

THE two previous drawings were strictly mountainous in character. I have now introduced one with trees of some size, and continued, in a slight degree, the practice of the former distances. Regard has also been had to the singleness of the subject, if I may use the term, in the hope of inducing many to seek out the like during the season for working out-of-doors. There are so many failures, attended by perplexity and disappointment, in the attempt to portray scenes of a difficult description, that I am desirous of leading the beginner to those of a simple kind; so that, when he has had practice in such, he may exercise his pencil upon subjects of greater combinations and importance. Success is always encouraging; failures invariably depressing. The former can only be attained when the ability is equal to the task; the latter is a sure evidence of incompetent skill. It is much more prudent to undertake too little than too much; because there is real pleasure in the pursuit of any accomplishment where the powers are not overtasked, and where we are influenced by confidence in place of fear. To the sketcher, CONFIDENCE is truly necessary; for, with this feeling, there will be both freedom and decision of touch, a clear and well-formed outline, a judicious arrangement of light and shade, and a perception of colour that will be in accordance with the landscape under treatment. Where the mind can fully comprehend the matter, a little patience and care will most assuredly carry out the work most satisfactorily. But if the matter is beyond the mind, then it is advisable never to hazard subjecting the latter to perplexity and disappointment. I have dwelt upon this at some length, knowing the folly of aiming at difficult subjects; and shall make a point, from time to time, of repeating the caution.

The present drawing is of simple materials;—sky, mountain, water, a hillside, a flat tract of middle distance and foreground, with a group of trees to the left, and a few stones bounding the watercourse to the right. In making the sketch, the water-line should be the first drawn; then the line for the middle distance below it, and the particular rising angle of the hillside. After these, draw the central mountain, carefully noticing its incidence upon the hillside, and the precise position of its greatest elevation. This must be found by an imaginary perpendicular line from it to the water; which line, in this instance, falls just upon the point whence the hillside rises from the valley. This practice is the only true method of finding the relative points of the several objects, and will prevent their being placed too far on either side. Of course, comparing by means of imaginary horizontal lines will insure the relative height of each object. The dark line at the further end of the foreground is now to be given; and the curvatures of the road, pathway, and watercourse on the right. Now, raise the stem of the nearest tree, and the exact position of its neighbours. In groups of this kind, the most perpendicular stem should always be drawn first; and then the direction of those near to it can easily be settled by the indication of a dot below, and another at the proper distance above and also at any part where there is a change of angle. This done, the outline can readily be filled in without hesitation. Attention in this respect will save much time. The stems being sketched in, the foliage can be placed with great truthfulness, and will appear to have a proper support.

TREES are felt to be very difficult to the amateur. "I cannot draw a tree," is constantly sounding in my ears; and this arises from a want of appreciation of the construction of stems, limbs, and foliage. There

E

is considerable arrangement in the clusters of branches, not only as affecting the outside of the tree, but also its interior; and it is upon a just perception of the chief of them that the general character of form will depend. When trees occupy a conspicuous position, it is imperative that their forms should be gracefully drawn, so that they may recommend themselves to the spectator. Otherwise, they fail to give interest or excite pleasure. It is, therefore, to the outside foliage and to the graceful curvature of lines—noting whence the foliage proceeds—that we must direct the special attention; afterwards filling in the clusters of hanging boughs in front of the stems. If this be well done, an agreeable effect will be produced; but if not, clusters or solid masses of impossible forms are very likely to present themselves. Of course every tree has a peculiar growth of its own, a knowledge of which can only be gained by drawing it from Nature, with the full determination to study its individual character, both of stem and foliage.

In the treatment of Grass there is also a general failure, and this I attribute to the same non-appreciation of form that we find in regard to foliage. Nothing conduces more to the effect of a picture than a pleasing distribution of patches of grass in the foreground. The colour they bear, in contrast to the ground whence they spring, naturally gives very decided features of form, and as these are so immediately in the front, they produce the greatest influence upon the eye, either for an agreeable impression or otherwise. An artist is so well aware of this fact, that he is often put to much trouble before he can produce a satisfactory arrangement; and not until he has done this, is he inclined to turn his attention to other portions of the work. In the accompanying drawing there is much practice of the kind, and it will be seen that, not only do the forms or direction of lines of grass undulate naturally, but that the several masses are also of different quantities and considerably varied in tone of colour. It is upon the outside lines of the grass that the forms of the road, the path, and the watercourse depend; so that here is another reason (and a very important one) for giving study and careful drawing to this part of the sketch.

The detached bits of Stone are, in their turn, useful by position, to direct the eye to the sides and centre; and this they do by assuming a crescent-like form round the foreground. The upright figure repeats the perpendicular lines of the trees.

There is but little actual light in the drawing, the general impression being that of half-tone, and the only positive dark is upon the figure, which, from its blue, red, and brown drapery, imparts a mildness of tint to all around. The highest or brightest yellow light is upon the centre of the distant vale, while the light stone to the left under the tree, and those by the watercourse to the right, invite attention to the entire foreground. I will only add, that where there is an absence of deep and powerful shadows, great judgment must of necessity be applied to balancing the warm and cool tints; and to this the student cannot too soon direct his attention.

The colours employed were, for the—

Sky—Cobalt.

Clouds—Sepia, cobalt, and a little lake.

Mountains—Cobalt, lake; yellow ochre, with a glazing of gamboge and raw sienna on the yellow part, raw sienna and lake on the red; and terre verte on the green parts.

Middle Distance—Raw sienna and yellow ochre for a first wash. Cobalt, lake, and raw sienna, for the markings. Raw sienna and lake for the spaces between; for the highest light, gamboge and lemon-yellow.

Trees and Grass—Gamboge, bright sienna, and indigo; a little sepia introduced for the dark shadows. A glazing of terre verte on parts of the greener tones.

Stems, and Shadows of Roads and Stones—Sepia, lake, indigo.

Light Tint of Road—Yellow ochre, lake, sepia.

AT LUSS, ON LOCH LOMOND.

THERE is a little deviation in this drawing from the out-door sketching, because I am desirous of combining the character of the three previous subjects, and so affording to many of my students an opportunity of putting into practice the several objects before noticed.

In this drawing there is scarcely anything but what may be deemed local, and that of such size as to give free scope for copying *forms* with literal correctness. I use the term "literal correctness," as rather implying a truthful impression, than that elaborate and minute attention to individual detail which is now generally understood by the word "Pre-Raphaelitism." Each portion of the cottages, for instance, is to be carefully drawn in with blacklead pencil, showing the various demarcations of thatch, wood, and stone. Nothing is more improving in a manipulative point of view, nor, indeed, in an intellectual one, than this kind of practice; for there must of necessity be much thought brought to bear on giving to each object and every part of it a veritableness of resemblance, so that there can be no mistaking the thing intended.

Over and over again do I hear the remark, "I thought it was not requisite to draw so much with the pencil, when there was colour to be put on." A greater mistake than this there cannot be, for if colour has to be used, it is essential that the precise position for it should be accurately marked and well drawn; inasmuch as the pencil is often of the greatest use in keeping up the crispness of outline definition. This cannot be too much insisted upon, it being by the pencil that the first impression has to be made and the foundation laid for success in after treatment. To each stone there is a form; to each branch there is a form; to each patch of grass there is a form; the chimney, the windows, the thatch, the old broken door, the boat, all have forms peculiarly their own; and it is only upon a just regard to each that they can be presented to the spectator in an intelligible and agreeable manner, and the end be at the same time attained of investing the scene—be it what it may—with a truthful character. I fear that some may think I have dwelt almost too much upon a careful pencil outline; but this is of such importance to a successful drawing, that it were far better I should appear too particular than not be particular enough; and I therefore repeat that nothing lies nearer the root of failure than a vague and hurried outline; while, on the other hand, an industrious and a carefully studied one is perhaps one of the greatest elements of success.

The present subject is given with great clearness of form throughout. The light and shade, as well as contrast of colour, are sufficiently pronounced to convey the idea of breadth, and at the same time to keep transparency in every part; that is, to give colour and depth without a tendency to blackness. The sky is of a cool grey, for the purpose of showing the warm colouring of the cottages to greater advantage. Whenever there are masses of tones inclining to orange, citrine, or red, it is necessary to have some corresponding masses of grey, in order to establish a requisite amount of repose and quiet; but these must be so treated as not to disturb or check the harmony by a suddenness of transition.

The dark tones of the clouds are repeated by the shadows on the mountain at the opposite side, the warm tints of which also repeat in a subdued degree the orange and laky hues of the thatch. These are again diffused over the walls of the cottages by the colours of the stones, and the grey shadows of the walls being warmer than the clouds, are adapted to cause them to advance, especially as the several glazings introduced are calculated to cause the eye to traverse over the whole breadth in an agreeable manner. It is on the decided edges of these shadows that the gleams of sunlight depend for their "catchy" vividness. The upturned boat, being separated from the cottages and the shadow of the road, partakes of the warm grey, so giving a second mass, although but a small one, and produces a circular form in the composition by its connection with the stony portion of the ground to the right. The highest light, which is to be found on the left cottage wall, between the window and the door, is caught up by the upper part of the post supporting the wall, and repeated on the figure of the woman over the boat, and again by the chimneys, and then passes off in the light of the sky. Indeed, every light—as every colour—has its purpose, and it would always be well that, when copying a drawing, the pupil should study it carefully in all its parts, and endeavour to discover the intention of the artist. The two bright "bits" of orange colour in the instance I have given serve to illumine the scene and carry force by contrast, although they are so small. The dark blue coat is also valuable to bring depth into the right portion of the picture, as well as to throw the background into distance. In the trees there is much variety of colour, light, shade, and form. I preferred massing the foliage, thinking it better to do so, and have only introduced a few slight branches at the right extremity to give lightness and to indicate the effect of wind upon them. The grass on either side is so marked in its several contours as to show the character of the ground upon which it grows. I have omitted any detailed account of the progressive "washings-in" of colour, having a desire to exercise the ability of the pupil in this respect; nevertheless, I subjoin a list of the combinations of the various tints to be employed—

CLOUDS—Cobalt, yellow ochre, and a little lake.

MOUNTAIN—Cobalt, lake, yellow ochre.

DISTANT TREES—Yellow ochre, cobalt, and a little lake, glazed with gamboge in the light parts.

NEAR TREES AND GRASS—Gamboge, burnt sienna, and indigo, varied.

THATCH—First Tint—Yellow ochre, lake, and cobalt, varied.

SHADOWS AND DEEP MARKINGS—Burnt sienna, lake, and indigo, with a little brown pink.

GLAZINGS OF YELLOW TONES—Raw sienna.

SHADOWS OF WALL AND ROAD—Burnt sienna, lake, and indigo, with glazings of burnt sienna, lake, and brown pink where required.

All the dark markings are touched in with the same colour, used thickly or in a pulpy condition. These touchings are of several depths, and can only be effected by a repetition; each being smaller in succession.

I would strongly recommend all who really wish to succeed in water-colours to copy this drawing more than once, it being calculated to afford improvement.

HUT AT GORPHWYSFA, NORTH WALES.

THE road from Capel Curig to Snowdon passes by the hotel at Pen-y-Grwyd, and thence taking a turn to the right (that to the left being to Beddgelert), ascends a hill of considerable length, the summit of which opens out to the tourist the wild and almost chaotic "pass of Llanberis." At this point there are a few poor huts or cottages with a comfortable little inn (a truly welcome one to travellers), taking the name of *Gorphwysfa*, or a resting-place. To the left of this, there is a lone hut at the entrance of the rudely constructed road or mountain track leading to the wondrous peak of Snowdon.

This hut forms the subject of my present illustration. Small and insignificant as it is, it has, from its desolate position, a character that impresses one with the idea of solemn dignity. It stands erect and solid in its stony construction; at the front of a vast arena of heights and depths, undulating and precipitous, full of the adjuncts of a mountain district, with huge masses of riven rocks occupying positions truly picturesque, and dispersed about—as well as disposed—in forms both grand and sublime. The lesser mountains (none can be called hills) are so distributed as to present so many prominent features in the scene, and from their barren and rocky heads being somewhat rounded, probably by glacier action in times gone by, they serve to give table-lands from whence the sides undulate more or less suddenly, and continuing their descent deeper and deeper, they at length rest their base on the narrow and beautiful vale of Nant Gwynant. From the other side of this lovely spot—and it is a lovely one—the mountains forming the group and extension of Moel Siabod take their rise, and a little way up can be seen the descending and winding road towards Beddgelert. These mountains are joined by other ranges, which assume every variety of direction and shape, rising one before another, and exhibiting rugged combinations of rock and herbage so diversified as to produce a constant change of colour. Thus they afford, as it were, fresh starting-points for more remote forms, until the eye rests upon outlines mingling with the clouds, connecting sky to earth, and producing an effect always grand, mysterious, and impressive. The lofty eminences to the right are the south-eastern buttresses or spurs of the Snowdon range. Nothing can be more picturesque than their sharp angular character; and either side being equally precipitous, the ridge is necessarily very narrow. The principal of these is named Lliwedd, a frowning steep, deeply furrowed and riven by blast and tempest, with a bleak and savage aspect, destitute of one redeeming point as to vegetation, save at the dipping of its base in the darkly toned waters of Llyn Llydaw, a wild and romantic lake about one and a half mile in length. The road or track to the right is exceedingly tortuous and hilly; and the large stones constantly rising in the centre make the drive anything but pleasant to those who are not in the habit of riding in cars almost without springs. I know no other locality where such exquisite combinations of foreground materials can be found. There is every characteristic that the sketcher can desire, and at times it is extremely difficult to settle which shall become the subject of the pencil. Patches of long and many-coloured grasses rise out of dark and purply blackened peat, contrasting with warm grey stones, which, moss-grown and lichened, lie side by side in every possible way, and of every imaginable shape. It is truly surprising to witness the eccentricities of colour—for I must use the term—to be found upon the same species of stone. Some partake of the orange, others of browns, russets, purples, and greys, of every shade and hue; while not a few are almost colourless and white. It is this that enables the artist frequently to bring the whole force of the palette into his foreground without having recourse to drapery or cattle.

In giving the above description, it of course must not be supposed to have reference to the drawing of the stone-built hut with the surrounding country, because it were folly indeed to give, in an elementary

F

work like this, a subject for imitation so comprehensive and poetic in its character; but it was introduced immediately on my return from a sketching tour in that locality (having made the solitary hotel at Pen-y-Gwryd my head-quarters), that I might lay before many a lover of the grand in Nature the multiplicity of exquisite subjects with which the vicinity of Snowdon abounds. My stay there was sadly too short, not one day being without rain, and yet this did not prevent the endeavour to bring back some study fraught with instruction and profit. It is impossible to be seated before scenery of such sublime proportions, without reflecting upon the wonderful manner in which its stupendous forms are brought together. What perfect arrangement there is in every successive change, and with what exquisite felicity the whole are grouped so as to charm the eye by never-ending variety of outline and construction—these may be better imagined than told. Sometimes the effect is solemn and portentous, with passing clouds that, hurried on by the wind, assume all manner of shapes, sweep over the higher portions of the landscape, and envelop the mountain-tops in the most mysterious manner. At other times a parting cloud lets in a flood of light, exhibiting ramifications of rock and a number of inequalities that were little suspected to exist; or some projection is brought into prominence by silvery streaks of light, displaying a vividness almost startling. Indeed, the effects in a mountainous district are so ever fresh and fugitive, that a note-book should always be at hand, to write down the lessons Nature so abundantly teaches; and if in the progress of one sketch attention is given to passing changes, that one sketch may be productive of several pictures. Colour, again, is another feature for study and observation, subject to alteration of atmosphere and power of light. Space has to be rendered truthfully; distance must be portrayed as distance, and all the intermediate objects, as they advance to the foreground, must keep their place, localising where they should localise, until colour is seen in all its unchanged character immediately in the front. Yes, it is impossible to sit down before scenery such as I have humbly endeavoured to describe without reflecting upon "the why and the wherefore," and striving to learn some lesson from the riches of the heights and depths of created Nature. I shall hope hereafter to speak of other scenes in my late tour, and trust they will recall to many who have gone over the same ground the degree of admiration they experienced during their sojourn amidst the mountains.

With the exception of the figures (and there were several looking over me while sketching), I have given the most simple and truthful representation of the hut and scenery that I possibly could. Not one stone has been added, and, I may say, not one has been omitted. Everything was carefully drawn with the blacklead pencil, and with some power of line, because, by so doing, less time would be spent in colouring. There was a place for everything; and every change of tint found its place most readily, and without hesitation. Even the sky was pencilled as well as the mountains and mid-distance. The road and its accompaniments, the grass and its undulatory character, were strictly drawn with the pencil. The large grey stone by the side in the second portion of the road was blasted and cut, as it completely stopped the way, so that it is a correct portrait. It is very remarkable that in no one instance in this locality did I perceive the roofs grown over with moss or grass of any kind; while in almost every other spot this is the general accompaniment of a cottage roof.

The colours employed were—for the

SKY—Light red, a little sepia, and indigo.

MOUNTAINS—Light red, a little sepia, and indigo.

MIDDLE DISTANCE—Lake, sepia, indigo, and yellow ochre; the first tone being of yellow ochre, lake, and a very little indigo.

THE HUT—Sepia, indigo, lake, gamboge, yellow ochre, in different proportions, sepia being the preponderating colour.

GRASS—Gamboge, burnt sienna, and indigo, for the warmer tints; gamboge, indigo, and a little sepia for the cool tints.

DEEP TOUCHES—Gamboge and sepia, throughout the foreground and building.

The whole of the colours are to be applied without any subsequent washings off. The time to be occupied in making such a sketch, out-of-doors, with the like degree of finish, should be from three to four hours; but if the careful outline with a black-lead pencil is not patiently carried out, five or even six hours will not suffice to produce a finished result.

CRUMMOCK WATER, CUMBERLAND.

No. I.

—◦◦◦◦—

THE first washes only are given in the present subject, that the pupil may be more easily initiated in the manner in which a water-colour drawing of this description is commenced.

The character of the finished work will always depend upon the under-tints, so that it is necessary to have them of a kind most favourable for the after-tones. I am not without hope that the example given may serve to show clearly what the appearance of the first stages of a drawing should be, and how it is to be obtained. As in all the previous subjects in this work, the pencil outline has been dwelt upon as the greatest help in producing a satisfactory result; so in the present illustration there must be the most careful attention in placing each individual formation in its right position; and not only in this, but in drawing it with freedom as well as accuracy.

One thing I invariably find the pupil not to pay sufficient regard to (although it may almost appear to many too trifling to notice), is the manner in which the pencil is cut. But there is more in this than most persons suppose. Without a true point, it is impossible, to judge correctly of the line to be produced. The wood should be much cut away in a slanting direction, to permit of the eye resting upon the point without interference. Neglect of this is frequently a cause of failure, and it is not an uncommon occurrence that a careless outline carries with it a corresponding manner throughout the colouring. It is to be hoped this caution may not pass unheeded, it being borne in mind that a *clear* line *directs* and a *blurred* line *confuses*, causing much hesitation in laying on the first (and generally large) washes of colour.

The Lake scene under treatment has been selected from its singleness of character, that is, from the masses being large, and their detailed formations easily seen. These have been drawn in with the black-lead pencil to secure the proper forms and position of the several shadows. All deviations from an even surface of ground should invariably be marked, as they serve to denote a variety of flowing, and (at times) continuous lines, and add greatly to the interest of the work. If the tree and foreground be equally regarded, the places for the different tints will be found with ease.

The outline being correct, pass some water over the whole with a large flat brush, and, while still damp, lay on a light wash of neutral orange or yellow ochre and brown madder, over the drawing, to impart a warm tint. This will also fix the pencilling and prevent its rubbing. When dry, again wash with water, and, as soon as the wet disappears, begin the upper portion of the sky with a tint of pure cobalt, carefully leaving the light clouds. Continue the wash by adding a little light red to produce a grey tone for the clouds, and deepen toward the lower edges with more cobalt. This operation should be effected at once; nevertheless, if it be too light, the tones may be subsequently strengthened. A tint of light red, yellow ochre, and cobalt, is to be mixed as nearly as possible to the colour of the warm portion of the mountain, and also a mixture of cobalt with a little indigo for the blue portion.

Commence at the top, with the brush tolerably well filled, carefully preserving the outline, bringing the colour from it into the body of the mountain; then, on nearing the bluer portion, add the mixture of cobalt and indigo, until the whole of the mountains are covered; softening the colour down to the lower edge, and *over* the warm tint for the low land and trees. This same blue tint is to be passed over the water, leaving the broad lights. The foreground stones of grey tints are now to be put in with cobalt and light red, varying the proportions to the character of tone required. After this, gamboge, light red, and cobalt, more or less of one than of the others, are to be employed for the herbage.

A very light tint of the first mixture, with more cobalt added, is now to be passed over the greyer parts of the warm colour, and the blue must be deepened with the cobalt and indigo. It will be seen that there is a warm tone on the dark mountains. This should have resulted from the blending of the first tints, by one running into the other while wet: but if the warmth is not sufficient, the first tint may be slightly passed over it again. The line of trees on the low land must now be washed in with yellow ochre, light red, and a little cobalt; also the rocky projection at the right. The shadows of the stem of the tree are of cobalt and light red, and when dry are to be deepened; use the same, only with more of light red; this tint is also to be employed for the dark stones. Gamboge and a little brown pink will give the colour for the foliage; after this, wash a tint of yellow ochre and light red for the colour of the stem, and, when dry, introduce the shadows and markings on the dark mountains with the cobalt and indigo, and then another wash of the same (more cobalt) on the second tints of the water.

It is recommended to do this drawing twice over, with a view of gaining manipulative dexterity; and having done so, to lay aside the copy and endeavour to reproduce it from *memory*. This is by far the best way to obtain a practical knowledge of colour, as it will enable the amateur to apply it to his own sketches.

CRUMMOCK WATER, CUMBERLAND.

No. II.

FULL instruction was given in the preceding drawing for the first washes of the Lake Scene, of which I now present the finished drawing. That it may be carried through without deviation from the first intention, I have worked upon the actual chromo-lithograph itself, carefully attending (with another impression before me) to every detail of pencilling, so that those persons who undertake to copy it may be enabled to continue the colouring without confusion or difference.

There is much softness and simplicity of treatment in the drawing—breadth being its characteristic. Therefore, when adding to it the warm grey shadows, all dark touches will have to be avoided, otherwise it will not exhibit that serene atmosphere for which our English Lakes are so deservedly renowned. Although *repose* constitutes the feeling of the scene, yet it is by no means wanting in variety either of form or colour. There is, indeed, much diversity—much for the eye to dwell upon, as it scans the broken surfaces of Red Pike on Crummock Water, and the High Style and Haycocks on Buttermere. It will now be seen how valuable those pencilled outlines have been in establishing truthfulness of form and position, giving to each spur of the mountains its true character and formation, so that the appropriate tints can be applied unhesitatingly to the several shadows of its component parts.

The clouds are touched upon with rose madder and indigo; the tint to be used very liquidly. After this is done, proceed to put in the shadowed side of the rocks on the near mountain (Red Pike), carefully following the pencilled outline. There are two degrees of shadow made with cobalt and rose madder, both of which are to be introduced *tenderly*. The greenish and isolated spur has a little yellow ochre mixed with the cobalt and rose madder; lake must be substituted for rose madder if the pupil has not the latter. A glazing—that is, a thin wash of colour—of raw sienna and a little gamboge is next to be put on the grassy surface, while, in the warmer parts, the tint is made with raw sienna and rose madder.

The distant mountains are principally shaded with indigo and cobalt, and the lighter spaces warmed with light tones of rose madder. The red tint also of the right portion of the mountain in light is obtained by one or two washes of rose madder over the first tints. Each of the divisional markings or forms will require strict attention, for the reasons that distances are determined by them.

The line of trees in the middle distance must now claim attention; and cobalt, with a little yellow ochre and Chinese white, be mixed for the grey shadows of their colours. The cobalt should be largely the predominant, and the less there be of the white the better, or the effect might be chalky. The warm tone and general character of the trees must be given by raw sienna, with a little cobalt and rose madder for the shadowy parts. In doing this, the forms should be gracefully given, without regularity of either shape or size. The treatment of such a passage as this is generally found by the learner to be difficult, because much taste, and even skill, is required to prevent stiffness. The rocky projection to the right is of cobalt, rose madder, and yellow ochre, with a little brown pink added for the darkest parts.

The foliage of the large fir-tree is done with a mixture of Indian yellow, burnt sienna, and indigo used in some substance. The forms are to be attended to very accurately, so that the clusters may fall into their several masses and take their proper shapes. The stem in its dark parts is deepened with brown madder and indigo, the touches being put on with decision. It is necessary to observe the breadth of light in this tree, or the general effect will be in danger. The deepest touches have burnt sienna added. Raw sienna and gamboge are employed for the grass in the foreground, with an occasional addition of indigo where the tone inclines to green rather than to citron. The several stones and rocks are cobalt, brown madder, and brown pink; the last colour only being required for the very warm and deep touches.

G

Yellow ochre and rose madder supply the orange tones, and also serve for the stem of the tree where it is of a light and warm hue. The markings or touches in the foreground must be placed at the extremity of the different tints, so as to impart clearness and brilliancy, and secure a crispness of effect.

The water should now have a warm wash of rose madder over the darkest side, and also at the front. When dry, two more washes of cobalt and a very little Chinese white are to be touched on horizontally, leaving the several lights. After this, go over the part from near to the boat with raw sienna and a little cobalt, to give a transparent tone, and with a little more raw sienna put on the few lines of ripples when the other is dry. The boat and figures are coloured with cobalt and light red, vermilion being added for the red coat. Indigo is for the cap of the foreground figure, and vermilion and rose madder, shaded with sepia, are mixed with reds for the coat.

The principal endeavour of the learner should be to keep the whole of the forms throughout, from first to last, *clearly defined*. I have been careful to give a subject for illustration that bears this stamp of manipulation, well knowing its importance, more especially in works intended for the portfolio. In this drawing the effect has been produced without any washing off, and is simply the result of laying on the colours with care and neatness.

A few words as to the design and construction of our drawing may be of much service in explaining how light and shadow, as well as contrast of tones, are dispersed systematically, so as to produce a pleasing balance of effect. The sky has in it but little actual blue, which will be found at the top to the left side; this softens into warm grey to the right, and deepens into a bluer tone as it reaches the mountains, while it weakens gradually into light broken clouds, interspersed with white on the lower part over the dark mountains. The water is the reverse of the sky, the dark side being under the light of it, and the light side under the dark clouds, so that the highest lights may be said to have exchanged places. This is also the case with the mountains. The breadth of warm colour on Red Pike is taken across the drawing on the foreground, and the blue tone of the mountains in contact with the light sky is, in a less degree, repeated in the darks of the line of trees, and the separate spurs at the bases of the large mountains. The breadth of warm colour is diffused over the distant foliage, and joins the foreground, which is brought to a focus upon the white bit of rock near the tree's foot, against which the figure is placed. As the principal weight of the drawing is in the tree and stones of the foreground to the left, it was requisite to give strength to the other side, only in a less degree, for which purpose the boat and depth of shadow on the rock were introduced, and they will be found to have given the balance sought. The foreground figure and the boat with figure serve to give a little animation to the scene as well as positive colour.

Believing this class of drawing to be more instructive than any other under the term of pure land-scape, I purpose to continue it, and in my next subject to pursue again the plan of treating the preparatory and the subsequent stages in separate papers.

A SPUR OF BEN LOMOND.

No. I.

THE effect of the present drawing is that of a summer's evening, when the sun has just sunk below the horizon, leaving the heavens illumined in softened, but still golden, light. At this particular time such an amount of warm reflection is diffused over the landscape as finds its way to the feelings of most people—at any rate, of all who are Nature-loving, and who delight in the study and practice of transmitting her effects to paper. We all like warmth of colour—it is natural to do so; there is something cheering and exciting in it; and for this reason, apart even from that mingling of harmonising and contrasting hues, a sunset effect is always looked upon with pleasure.

To give a simple, yet agreeable illustration, I have avoided any complicated arrangement of clouds, whereby the pupil would be confused, and have sought to produce a breadth of effect and singleness of character which will tend to show the blending of the tones peculiar to the *sunset*. I have also selected for study a description of scenery calculated to convey instruction and manipulative dexterity—the latter being requisite, truly requisite, for the expression of INTENTION. And this being the case, I cannot advocate too much a neat and careful method of handling the brush, or a careful study, before applying it, of what has to be done, and of the manner in which it is to be done. A little halting, with some thought upon "the why and the wherefore," will greatly help to success, whereas the want of it will always be accompanied by failure. An esteemed friend of mine, who really is an excellent amateur artist, once told me that immediately he began to put on the first wash of the sky, it was "a case of *sal volatile*, he felt so nervous." That this is a general feeling I can pretty well testify, having witnessed it so constantly in my numerous pupils; therefore I the more earnestly recommend the exercise of thought, first upon the *matter*, and then upon the *manner*, of treating it. In addition to all this, cleanliness is most desirable, and should be observed in respect to the Colour-box, Brushes, and Paper. The first should (at least in my opinion) always be sponged clean, and wiped with a palette cloth after finishing the day's painting. It will then be ready for further use, and the most delicate tints may be produced without danger of unnecessary mixture. The brushes should also be washed and put into form by passing them through the palette cloth. As for the paper, too great care cannot be taken in keeping its surface free from dirt or abrasion of any kind; and, to preserve the equality of texture, bread will be found preferable to india-rubber in making corrections. With these prefatory remarks, I begin to place before the amateur directions for copying the present subject upon Loch Lomond. It is only in the first stages of progression, and yet sufficiently coloured to give a somewhat true and pleasing impression.

I have said much—but not too much—upon the necessity of having a correct and well-drawn outline before thinking of commencing to colour. I will now only say, let it not be neglected. After the paper has been washed with clean water and a large brush, prepare some rose madder (or crimson lake) and yellow ochre in two different tints—the one inclining to a roseate hue and the other to a light amber; and, while the drawing is still damp, commence at the top with the red tint and join the yellow midway, then add the red just above the mountains, and also over them as far as the water, where again change for the yellow, passing over the middle distance and foreground to the right, and then again taking more red over the immediate front. While in its wet condition, take a piece of blotting-paper, folded once or twice, and touch with its sharp edge upon the white light on the stones by the water's edge, which will remove the colour very softly, and regain the white of the paper. This method of obtaining light is frequently put into practice when fleecy clouds or a mackerel sky are to be represented. When this first blotting in (or washing in) of colour is dry—quite dry—the drawing should be turned upside down, and the yellow portion of the sky passed over with clean water, and then a tint of cobalt, with a little rose madder (or lake) introduced into it, and carried to the top of the sky. This will give the grey warmth of tone seen above. After this, make some tints of the amber, roseate, and blue hues, and apply them over the mountains, observing where the several changes occur. Take care not to let the blue mingle with the orange tone, which would completely spoil the purity of colour, but let it rather amalgamate with the roseate tint, where it will unite agreeably into the soft clear greys, away from the influence of sunlight. Attention to these contrasting as well as harmonising varieties must be observed, as by them the effect of lustrous light, if I may so speak, is preserved. The water will also receive light washes from these colours. The warm yellow tones of the middle distance, as well as the grass, are to be put in with yellow ochre and a little rose madder. The grey shadows (warm in character) must also have their first washes placed correctly, and somewhat strongly, with the edges decided and clear.

At this stage, when the whole of the above flat tints are satisfactorily done, it is desirable to wash all over them with a soft brush and clean water, to remove the colouring matter from the upper surface of the paper. If properly washed, scarcely any of the colour will come off; nor should it, the object being simply to produce a more perfect blending, and to adapt the paper better to receive every subsequent wash. I find the safer plan to do this successfully is to place the drawing a short time before the fire, so that the colour may become hardened, and have some hold upon the paper, and then the washing may generally be depended upon. Different papers, however, have much to do in this respect, as well as the granulation of surface. A very fine texture, much sized, does not absorb the colour so well as a more open grain with less size: therefore too smooth a surface should be avoided. On the other hand, too rough a grain will not admit of the brush giving that clear and decided handling so much to be desired— at all events, by the tyro—in water-colour painting.

The washing having been accomplished, other tones have to be passed over the mountains (and sky if too light), with precisely the same colours, giving to each part the tint of which it partakes. The trees in the middle distance are of a variety of tones, produced from cobalt, yellow ochre, and crimson lake (not rose madder). For the middle distance and grass in the foreground use gamboge, raw sienna, and sepia. The stones are also continued in their darker touches and shadows with cobalt, yellow ochre, and lake, which colours are also to be employed for the stems of the trees. In the foliage of the nearer trees there is much diversity, and it is requisite to observe the exact character of the green tints, giving them precisely according to the copy, as their position is of much value to the effect of the whole drawing. Gamboge, burnt sienna, and indigo, with the addition of lake for one of them, are to be the colours for these several gradations or varieties of hues. The brush should be tolerably well filled for putting in these washes. The road is to have a slight wash of cobalt and rose madder over the front part, in order to send the light upon it to that part by the trees.

Beyond the foregoing instructions I say nothing, thinking it as well that, in the more immediate details, the pupil had better exercise the knowledge already attained. The same drawing in its finished state will form our next subject, and will be fully explained in all its details.

A SPUR OF BEN LOMOND.

No. II.

THE few forms of which this subject is composed are much varied in respect of lines, every portion of them partaking of undulations, with the exception of the central spur of Ben Lomond and the several detached and fallen rocks from the water's brink. The serpentine outlines of the many divisions of grassy mounds seem to play into each other in easy and graceful contours, while, at the same time, they admit of considerable alternation of light, shade, and colour. Opposed to them are the perpendicular trees, which rise in some significant height before the background, and convey to it the idea of softened and hazy atmosphere. Their stems are all of different length, breadth, and inclination, thereby affording little chance of formality. The position of each stem at its junction with the ground will be found to bear the line of beauty, and help to show the several progressive stages of distance in their immediate locality. This point is seldom attended to with the proper degree of thought or care that it ought, although by a due observance of the varied lines of a foreground, the eye is led on step by step until it finds itself carried into the middle distance, and, receding still further, becomes lost in a far-off haze.

This mingling is often the result of well-disposed lines, growing, as it were, out of each other, and so skilfully intertwined that none but the artist would suppose the effect could proceed from such a primitive cause. It is nevertheless perfectly true that distance is frequently more the result of lines than of colour, although, of course, the latter must ever be the true interpreter of the former. The groups of trees at the end of the loch are also of different sizes and forms, but so managed as to carry out the flowing undulations in the composition of lines. This is obtained by having reference to the several heights, to which particular attention is called. The stones at the water's edge in the foreground are arranged somewhat in the form of an ellipse, and yet so varied in size and form as to preclude the possibility of such an impression. The angular shape of the central mountain is, by contrast to the curved lines below, made to rise up with increased grandeur, and is suggestive of bleak and rugged wildness. Its height is made more apparent from the trees by the water, over the stones, being placed immediately underneath the summit, thus giving its full dimensions from the base. The dark, or rather blue range of hills below, in front, assist by their continuity in giving a certain impressiveness to the one solid mass; while the outline of the distant mountain, so different in character, still adds to the precipitous and rocky steeps of the principal object of interest. One particular more I would wish to be well noticed, and that is the form of the long soft cloud above the mountain. If it were of any other shape than it is, it would necessarily have attracted undue attention, whereas by its simple, though slightly broken horizontal line, both mountains have their peculiarities strongly and clearly developed. Thus far have I thought it necessary to speak of the manner in which the several lines of the picture are composed, and how these in their varieties obtain value the one from the other. It is from the want of study in this individual branch of the art that much real pleasure in the contemplation of Nature or of a picture is lost. The intention in the working out of the scene too frequently escapes general observers, who, as a rule, do not imagine for one moment that the principles of art run so deep as to call forth the most intense efforts of the mind before they can be presented in all their excellence, and convey a just and reasonable idea of Nature—of Nature under her many garbs—of Nature in her numberless and varied effects.

With regard to colour, a general warmth pervades the whole drawing, which is cheered by the line of small blue hills in the middle distance. This blue tint must not be too suddenly introduced, otherwise it would be *unharmonising*, if I may use the term; but rather should it be insinuated upon the purply tone of which the general mass of shadow is composed. This blue tone is also carried into the lower and

M

shadowed portions of the trees, and in a less cold degree upon the rocks. I have said less *cold* degree, which means that there should be a little *red* added (crimson lake). The presence of the white stone in the foreground is very necessary to give depth of tone to the other light portions of the drawing; indeed, all high lights are of the greatest importance, as well as all the deepest touches, because they form so many points of attraction, upon which the eye will be sure to rest.

In carrying the colouring of this subject to completion, the sky should receive the line of cloud with a soft yet decided edge, as this will give considerable space beyond the mountains. There are two tones of clouds at the top edge, being of yellow ochre and rose madder, and that about the mountains partaking of more rose madder and a very small portion of cobalt. These tints may be passed over the mountains. After they are dry, the broad shadows upon the mountains are to be washed on with a thin colour, made of cobalt and rose madder, carrying it under the blue tones; and, while it is drying, it will be advisable to put on the horizontal tints upon the water with the same colour. The next thing to be done should be the more detailed shadows on the mountain, and afterwards the blue tones of the low line of hills, which should be of cobalt, a very little gamboge, and Chinese white, the gamboge being to impart a slight green tone to the blue, and the Chinese white to give a little opacity, in order that it may show more readily over the under tints. The warm citrine tints of the grass are of raw sienna, mixed with rose madder in the redder parts, and a little cobalt where of a greener hue. All the trees in the middle distance are a modification of gamboge, lake, and cobalt, and will require careful painting; their reflections are put in with the same. The foreground trees are to have the markings of the clusters of foliage distinctly put on with gamboge, burnt sienna, and indigo, the brush being held rather uprightly, and the colour imparted by lifting the hand at each touch from off the paper, for the purpose of causing the forms to show out with decision and crispness; for nothing ought to appear blurred or softened. When the whole of these forms are given satisfactorily, the intermediate spaces are to receive their washes, being careful to leave such lights as are requisite, otherwise there will not be any gradation. For the two yellowish trees, gamboge, burnt sienna, and indigo are to be employed, varying the quantity of each according to the proper tint. The centre tree is shaded with cobalt, and lake over the first tint. A little cobalt and lake may also be put over the deepest shadows of the others, to impart a slight grey tone. In like manner the darkest touches are given upon the grass, and a few lines upon the water, keeping them horizontal. These are intended to represent the surface of the water.

It would be far more profitable to recommence this subject entirely, following out the directions given in the last lesson, and only having the former chromo-lithograph as a guide rather than making it the copy. In adopting this method the learner will, in time, better comprehend how all finished water-colour drawings are begun and carried through to completion.

STUDY OF STONES ON THE NORTH SIDE OF TALIARIS, NEAR LLANDILO, SOUTH WALES.

THERE are few details in the foreground of a picture of more value to its effect than detached groups of stones, large or small. In no other objects do we find greater diversity of colour, although composed of the same material; and it is quite true that, although masses from the parent rock lie side by side, yet each and all vary in tint to an extraordinary degree. This offers us every desirable change of tone whereby our foreground can be enriched; and groupings of stones are no less valuable for the introduction of colour than for the distribution of light and shadow; for, being often the medium of some concentrated light, they become, as it were, the key-tone or focus of a whole drawing. This, however, will depend greatly, or, I should rather say, *entirely* on the character of the object. The introduction into a scene of large stones (fallen or surface stones) should always be the result of knowledge as to their possibility of getting there; and I mention this from the fact of their sometimes being a kind of stereotyped adjunct to a foreground, quite irrespective of the geological character of the site. This is an error so common, that the artist can at once detect between a truthful sketch and a tricky deception practised by a tyro. It matters little what the subject may represent, if there be a strict adherence to reasonableness throughout without bringing into notice any foreign objects totally at variance with the scene. Nothing shows greater ignorance than this; and I feel it would be an omission on my part, were I not to give a word of caution against so great an error.

The group of stones given for our subject is a part only of a sketch drawn and coloured on the spot. It will be found to combine variety of angular forms, and much diversity of colour, as well as great force of light and shade. In drawing groups, or even single stones, of this description, great attention should be paid to the general outline, and the several angles which are presented, to secure an appearance of a broken surface and of stone-like fracture. In almost every instance there must be a crispness of edge to each part, without softening or melting of one into the other. However slight the washes may be in the lightest parts, yet they must all have clear and decided edges. Indeed, if they do not, the consequence will be a resemblance to dough or putty instead of to stones. It is also of great importance that the breakage of divided portions should be properly and very attentively cared for, inasmuch as this is peculiar to each class of stone.

In a subject so local as this I have selected, I shall not enter into minute detail as to its stages of progression, but would remark that the principal thing to be observed throughout is to leave the whole of the lights clean, sharp, and well defined. To effect this, a true pencil outline is imperative; without it there cannot be a successful result. As regards the colouring, the student must determine those parts that are warm and those that are cold, that is, which tones are inclining to the yellow, orange, red, lake-purple, or blue-purple, to grey or blue. It is only by a true balance of each that an agreeable impression can be made, so that it is to be hoped this matter will have some consideration before commencing with the colour. The sky is produced simply with cobalt and a little lake. The light tints on the stones are obtained with yellow ochre, burnt sienna, lake, and cobalt, in different proportions, agreeable to the tint required. All the shadows are done with burnt sienna, lake, and indigo, varied, and a little gamboge introduced where the deepest touches are seen, because it causes the other colours to hold out with greater power from its being a natural gum and having a glossy quality. The herbage is a mixture of gamboge, burnt sienna, and indigo, more or less of one than the other, and lake introduced upon the indications of heather. The top of the hill and the small loose stones must be coloured with cobalt and light red, and the short grass of yellowish tone is of yellow ochre, and brown pink, and in the greener parts a little indigo added.

The foregoing instructions will be found sufficient to enable the learner to copy with accuracy the subject before him. I have introduced it into these pages for the purpose of giving an insight into the manner of portraying masses of fallen stone, thinking that in the season for sketching from Nature, many might wish to know where to meet with scenes of beauty, grandeur, and interest.

I am anxious to inform the student that in the chromo-lithograph there are, at times, numberless small specks, arising from the fact of the several tints being obtained from a point of lithographic chalk instead of by flat washes put on with the brush. It is a defect that cannot be entirely overcome, where there is any gradation of tint to be given; so that, when they are seen to exist in a sky or elsewhere, they must be regarded as meaning to convey the idea of so many flat tints, and should be copied simply as such. There is, however, an improvement even in this; and I am constantly impressing upon the mind of the artists who copy my drawings upon stone how requisite it is that this granular character should be overcome, it being likely to mislead those who are desirous of profiting by the several studies presented to them.

I have thought it as well to bring the above remarks before those persons who may copy these drawings, in order to remove any false impression they may have entertained upon the subject.

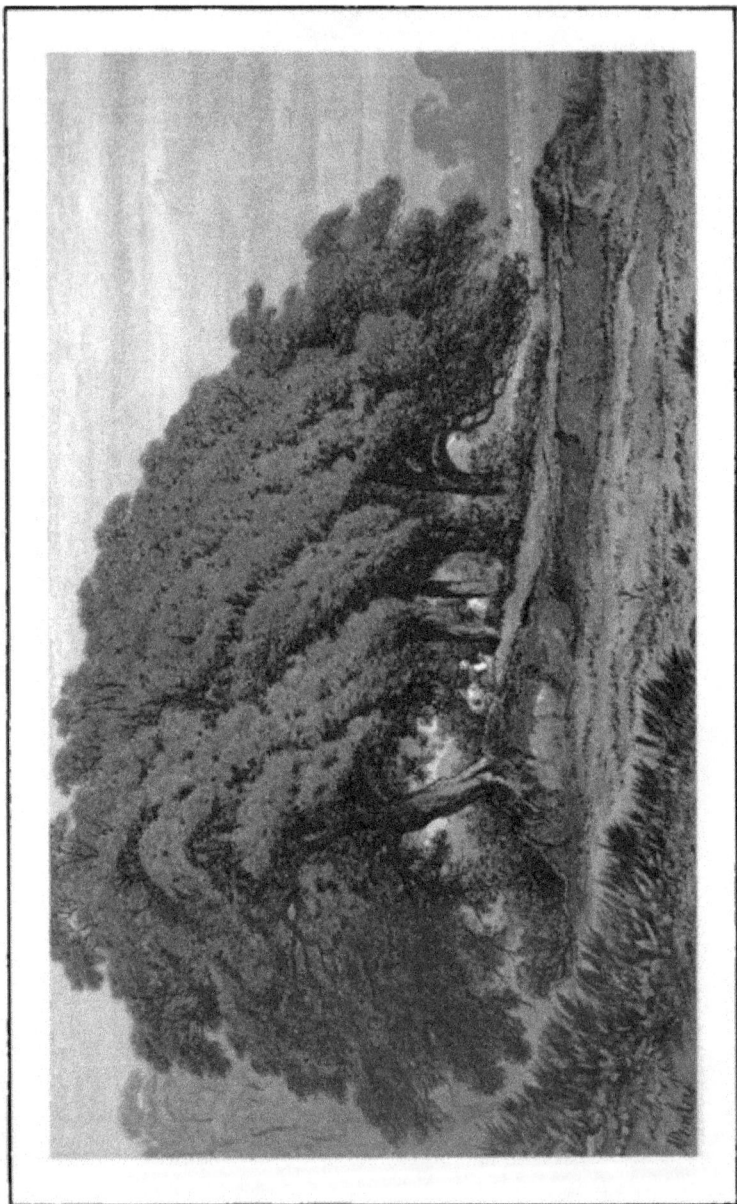

STUDY OF A GROUP OF OAK TREES, NEAR
ELTHAM, KENT.

THERE are few spots to be found of a more secluded and rustic character than are to be met with in some of the nooks and lanes of the suburbs of London, ranging from a distance of seven to ten miles. They are so retired, and have so much of the character of the country, that they cannot in any way be upbraided with the term "Cockneyism." To the amateur, it is a great boon that our vast and smoky metropolis abounds in local bits of the most desirable and charming kind, exquisitely suited for the pencil, and so retired as to permit of uninterrupted quiet in sketching, without the rude and ofttimes impertinent gaze of the passer-by. Such a spot was the subject now before us. About one mile from Eltham, in a lane turning to the left, and through the village, I came, with a few friends, upon some beautiful little artistic bits, refreshing to the mind as well as to the eye. Many there are who, after the duties of the day are ended, might put themselves into the train, and soon reach scenes of repose and tranquillity of the most enjoyable and rustic character. I can with safety recommend those who are fond of sketching to visit the locality of Beckenham, Bickley, Chislehurst, and Eltham, each of which can be reached in a very short time from the railway stations.

The trees in the present sketch group together in perfect form, round-headed and graceful, affording a mass of foliage well calculated to teach the student. Although the outside is symmetrical in shape, yet the few protruding branches are quite sufficient to break the otherwise circular outline, and give an agreeable impression. In sketching this and other similar trees, the first thing to be done should be to place some dots upon the paper, for the position of the bases of the several trunks or stems. Care should be taken to give these at correct distances the one from the other, or the whole will be thrown out of drawing when the foliage is outlined. The direction of inclination is now to be accurately observed, as well as the precise thickness of each, as upon the former will depend the whole growth of the foliage. The branches are to be continued to the top of the tree, noting well the highest part, and see that the several clusters of leafage are well supported. This is but seldom achieved by the student, and the trees necessarily assume an unnatural look. Let all the principal masses have an outline, and, indeed, a slight degree of pencilling in the shadows, because, if these are successfully done, it enables the artist to leave off and change his colour, when he would otherwise find it almost impossible to do so. This will prevent haste and fear of the colour drying before completing the first flat wash.

The outline of the bank should be well attended to, by observing the several breaks and direction of the grass at the top. There is a nice play of line on this bank, and also on the grass below, with the narrow pathway; while the weedy foreground to the left leads the eye up to the dark side of the foliage, continuing the shadow of the bushes under the trees, and giving to them an agreeable curve. Opposed to these varied lines is the horizontal meadow beyond, with a gleam of sunlight, backed by distant trees in grey tone. The ash-tree to the left, behind the principal oak-tree, is of a tender green, well suited to give firmness and strength of colour to the whole group in front. For this purpose also are the delicate grassy tints below of the greatest use, as their freshness and coolness impart by contrast considerable warmth of colour. The point of interest lies in the gravelly bank and large tree, upon which the high light falls. The stem receives the strongest light, which is carried forward by means of the sleeves and caps of the figures. Without the introduction of these the light would be too small, and the top form of it would rest upon the bank; whereas the presence of the figures gives a rounded character to the lights, and fills up a

1

gap not very interesting in itself. The orange and lilac colours are of great value in bringing colour to assist the concentration of light, and as a set-off or foil to the large masses of green. Perhaps there is nothing more difficult to compete with than these large surfaces of a greenish hue; and this being the case, it is imperative that the variety of tints of which this hue is composed should have our greatest study, that we may endeavour to avoid an unpleasant monotone. I have mentioned this to lead the pupil to be particular in imitating the several changes of tint throughout the drawing. The sky is composed of cobalt for the upper part, and a grey of cobalt, lake, and yellow ochre for the lower, carrying it over the distant trees, and changing it into yellow ochre for the meadow and grass in front. The foliage has a good strong wash of gamboge, burnt sienna, and indigo, leaving the few white places where the sky is seen. The same colours, used with more water, are to be applied on the grass, varying according to the required tints. After this, give a light tone of burnt sienna and a little yellow ochre over the gravelly bank and pathway; then take a tint of burnt sienna, lake, and indigo, and put on the stems of the trees. The distant trees are cobalt and lake, with a very small addition of gamboge. All the shadows of the gravelly bank are indigo, lake, and burnt sienna, using more of the last at the right end of the bank. It is requisite to wash the sky once after the first colours are on with clear water, and when dry to repeat the tints. Without this there would be no softness of atmosphere. The distant trees are likewise to be washed, although but slightly.

In painting masses of foliage that have depth of colour, it is absolutely necessary to put on several layers of tones, getting smaller each time. These have generally to be touched on, more by way of dabbing that any particular touching or manipulation. Nevertheless, the greatest regard must be had in preserving the outside forms of the inner clusters, so as to give their separations clearly and distinctly. All these constitute form, and as such should be carefully wrought out. The same colours are continued throughout, with the exception of a little French blue and lake being touched over the shadowed side at the last, to give a slight grey character to it. The trunks and branches are all strengthened with burnt sienna, lake, and indigo, using the colours thickly, and holding the brush well up to its point to ensure the sharpness of the touches. Of course the long grass will have to be varied in colour, but not very much at the first, because when the several tufts are placed in they can be tinted upon separately, and the different hues obtained in that manner. The very deep touches of dark must not be given at random, because all those are placed exactly in the proper position for leading the eye to them, and rendering all the intermediate spaces in half-tones, and so giving breadth. I put the figures in at the last with Chinese white, upon which I gave the different colours. Lake and cobalt for the lilac, vermilion for the scarlet, rose madder for the red handkerchief, and Indian yellow for the third figure.

It is for the benefit of many students who are unable to sketch mountain or lake scenery, that I have introduced this simple subject, there being scarcely any rural districts where groups of a similar character may not be found. I hope most sincerely it may be to the improvement of many, and lead them to search for beauties near home, without feeling that they are only to be found at a distance.

SCENE BETWEEN CAPEL CURIG AND LLYN OGWEN,
AT THE HEAD OF NANT FRANGON, N. W.

A MORE wild and dreary walk can scarcely be conceived than that from which our subject is taken; and yet there is a grandeur along the whole of the road, owing to the many huge mountain masses by which it is surrounded. I well remember this spot, and the degree of awe it inspired. Vast wastes of land, with upheaved stones rising from the surface almost at every step, mingled with peat, moss, and blackened soil, served to make up the landscape in a most striking, uncommon, and effective manner. How bleak it is at times those alone can tell who have encountered its violent gusts of wind and driving rain, from which it is in vain to seek for shelter. With all this severity, the artist shrinks not from venturing out to catch these lessons of storm, so calculated to give increased interest and sublimity to the efforts of his pencil. The passing cloud, overshadowing those huge forms in its course, is ever fertile in producing change, and offering suggestions of a pictorial character, each of which is laid up in memory's storehouse, to be placed at some future day upon canvas or paper. The sun's vivid gleam escaping from its cloudy prison, alights alternately upon each lofty and bare-headed summit, giving them such concentrated prominence that seems to bury all else in mysterious gloom, producing a breadth of effect that could not otherwise have been imagined. It is in the presence of Nature alone that the student's ideas can be formed, enlarged, and elevated. From constant converse with her the mind is led to reflect upon the beautiful and the grand, from which to gather scenic knowledge, and thus bring Art to bear upon it. Laws of light, laws of shadow, laws of perspective, are alone to be gleaned from studious observation; but when once they are so gleaned, how great is the reward for all the trouble taken! The result is certainly well worth the cost.

In the present subject, the foreground lies high, and the eye just discerns a peep of Llyn Ogwen with its background of mountain. The left of the view is occupied by forms of some magnitude before reaching the celebrated and sterile Trifaen. A barren and naked stamp pervades the whole landscape, although the diversity of tint and colour afforded by different grasses, peats, and masses of stone, serves to satisfy the spectator by its variety. A sameness there cannot be, and more especially when parts are partially concealed by shadow and other features are bathed in sunshine. There is a constant play of colour over the hoar masses of grey, of which our illustration is chiefly composed, which is repeated in greater brilliancy upon the herbage of the foreground. The grey sides of the large stones, by their depth of tone, serve to throw the mountains into distance, and impart aërial tones to them that without this extra power would scarcely have been felt; while the high lights they receive, and the broad mass of soft tints upon the road, are calculated to reduce the half-tones of the mountains, and to bring the white edges of the clouds into the immediate front. For this purpose the single sheep is placed at the bottom of the drawing, and also those at the far end of the bank. By carefully looking at this treatment, it will be seen that the eye is led round the drawing by means of tender half-shade, that the whole may be encircled. The heavy cloud helps to do this, and the straight portion of it shows out the several marked outlines of the mountains more distinctly by contrast. To every portion of the scene there are continuous lines of distance, all of which are of great value to show the position and surface of the separate masses. These can only be given by a succession of washes, one after the other, preserving the sharpness and decision of each. There must also be a preconceived intention to every touch or wash, in order that none of them be meaningless or vague. It is in this that the pupil differs from the accomplished artist, a result which is mainly to be attributed to the thoughtlessness of the one and the thoughtful study of the other. Whatever may be the object to be treated, be well assured that it is dependent upon details peculiarly its own, and should be regarded with attention and study. Perhaps there is greater difficulty in the present subject than in any previous one, owing to quantity of half-shadow being so pronounced upon by varieties of form as well as colour. It is scarcely possible to deal with these changes without washing the tint laid on two or three times with clean water, to remove the upper surface, and then glazing upon them with their tints of appropriate colours. The hanging cloud is done while the paper is wet, on account of the softness of the edges, and the straighter portion of it when dry, or nearly so.

I shall not enter into the manipulation of every part, having spoken at some length of the conception, working, and arrangement of the scene, with the earnest hope of leading all who copy it to throw their mind into reflections of a similar nature.

SKY—French Blue.

DISTANT AND NEAR MOUNTAINS—French Blue, Lake, and Yellow Ochre.

TINT OF ROAD—Yellow Ochre, Lake, and French Blue.

CLOUDS—Indigo and Blue Black.

STONES IN FOREGROUND—French Blue, Lake, and Yellow Ochre.

DEEPEST TOUCHES IN THE FOREGROUND—Burnt Sienna, Lake, and French Blue.

The whole of the above will require several different washes of colour; but it is useless to begin with the detail until a certain amount of depth is obtained in the grey tints. When attained, the whole of the upper tints may be given; and to do this well will require considerable skill, otherwise the effect is likely to become spotty and crude. Every wash must be decided and clear throughout.

YELLOW OCHRE, with GAMBOGE and LAKE, may be employed for the finishing warm tones. The same, with COBALT, omitting the yellow ochre, for the greener and brighter tints; and BROWN PINK must be added for the brightest colouring in the foreground. As there is much diversity of colouring, so must the respective tints be given in their proper places, noting where they partake of cool green, where of brown green, and where of the yellow and orange hues. Transparency must be the aim of the pupil, which will depend upon first obtaining a good ground of grey tones upon which to work, and then introducing every gradation of colour as required.